TITLE I

Contemporary African Americans

WALTER DEAN MYERS

BY
DIANE PATRICK-WEXLER

RSVP
RAINTREE
STECK-VAUGHN
PUBLISHERS
The Steck-Vaughn Company

Austin, Texas

Published by Raintree Steck-Vaughn, an imprint of Steck-Vaughn Company.
Produced by Mega-Books, Inc.
Design and Art Direction by Michaelis/Carpelis Design Associates.
Cover photo: John Craig

Library of Congress Cataloging-in-Publication Data
Patrick-Wexler, Diane.
   Walter Dean Myers/by Diane Patrick-Wexler.
      p.   cm.—(Contemporary African Americans)
   Includes bibliographical references (p.   ) and index.
   Summary: Presents the life and career of the Afro-American who grew up listening to stories and who carries on the storytelling tradition in his numerous and award-winning books.
   ISBN 0-8172-3979-0 (Hardcover)
   ISBN 0-8114-9796-8 (Softcover)
   1. Myers, Walter Dean, 1937—Biography—Juvenile literature. 2. Afro-American authors—20th century—Biography—Juvenile literature. [1. Myers, Walter Dean, 1937-   . 2. Authors, American. 3. Afro-Americans—Biography.] I. Title. II. Series.
PS3563.Y48Z83 1995
813'.54—dc20
[B]
                                                                    95-19550
                                                                    CIP
                                                                    AC
Printed and bound in the United States.

1 2 3 4 5 6 7 8 9 LB 99 98 97 96 95

Photo credits: John Craig: pp. 4, 38, 45; UPI/Bettmann: p. 7, Courtesy Walter Dean Myers: pp. 8, 11, 12, 17, 18, 23, 24, 27, 28, 32, 41; AP/Wide World Photos: p. 15; Angel Franco/NYT Pictures: p. 21, Courtesy Steck-Vaughn Company: p. 31; Harper & Row, Publishers, Inc.: p. 35, 42; Courtesy Scholastic Inc.: p. 36.

Contents

Chapter

IT SOUNDS TOO REAL!

"**O**nce upon a time,..." For young Walter Dean Myers, these words meant that his foster father Herbert Dean was getting ready to tell a story. When Walter heard these words, he could not decide whether to run and hide or hop on his father's lap and listen. It was not that the stories were boring. His father was a great storyteller. In fact, that was the problem! All the stories Herbert Dean told young Walter were scary. He told them so well that Walter would start looking around the room for monsters and other huge, frightening creatures.

From their apartment in New York City's Harlem, Walter's foster father could take Walter to faraway

Today, Walter Dean Myers is one of the foremost African-American writers of books for young people. His books are part of a tradition of storytelling passed down by his family and his community.

places. Herbert did this using only his voice and his imagination. Walter would close his eyes as he listened to his foster father speak. Suddenly, instead of being in their living room, Herbert and Walter would be in a haunted house or a sinking boat. Some stories were so real that Walter would get up and run out of the room. Even though he ran, one thing is for sure. Walter never forgot those stories.

It is no surprise, then, that Walter Dean Myers became a storyteller himself. Walter did not share his stories with just one child. Instead, he put his stories on paper, so that many people could read them. Walter began writing when he was ten years old, and he has never stopped.

When Walter was in school, he loved to read as well as write. But he found that there were very few books about African-American children like himself. He never read about children who lived in Harlem or in other mostly black communities. He never read about children who grew up with the experience of being African-American. Black children like Walter could not see themselves in books. Their stories were not being told.

When he became a writer, Walter Dean Myers decided that he would write stories about young black people. He would set his stories in Harlem, the place he knew best and loved most.

What would happen in the stories? Walter Dean Myers looked to his own life for the answer. Walter

Walter Dean Myers writes books that reflect the life experiences of young African Americans. Many are set in communities like Harlem, where the author grew up during the 1940s and 1950s.

remembered the hardships and the joys of the Harlem community. Many people there were tough and street-wise, but they were also very caring. Life there was not the same as it was in the books Walter read about white children. But the experiences—playing in apartment buildings, alleys, and church basements—were just as real. Walter felt it was important to tell stories that black children could relate to. He also believed it was important to write books for and about teenagers. Walter wanted his books to open up the world of possibility for young African Americans.

In his long career, Walter Dean Myers has written **nonfiction** and all types of **fiction**. His work includes realistic stories, fairy tales, ghost stories, and adventure stories. Some of his stories take readers to faraway places he has been to himself, such as Africa and South America. Sports, especially basketball, have been another popular subject for Walter because he has played and loved basketball since he was a child. Walter is also a lover of history, so some of his stories are set in ancient times.

Like his foster father, Walter Dean Myers can make a story so real that readers travel in their minds to the place he is describing. In fact, Walter's stories are so

Some Walter Dean Myers books are set in faraway places that he himself has visited. Here, he visits Rome, Italy, with his son Michael.

popular that young readers write letters to him all the time. Most of the letters thank Walter for making the characters in his stories sound real. Readers can see themselves in the characters. This is because Myers uses the language his readers use. He talks about the problems they have and uses young African Americans as models for his characters.

Have you ever read a Walter Dean Myers story? If not, you have a lot of wonderful reading ahead of you. Since 1969, Walter has written almost fifty **picture books** (for young children) and **novels** (for teens). Just the titles of some of the books might make you feel curious enough to read them: *The Dragon Takes a Wife*; *Fast Sam, Cool Clyde, and Stuff*; *The Legend of Tarik*; *Scorpions*; *The Righteous Revenge of Artemis Bonner*.

Which one would you choose first? Whatever your choice, one thing is certain. When you pick up a book by Walter Dean Myers, you pick up history. Between its covers might lie the world of Harlem, where teenagers fight for friendship and against racism. Or you might find a young African-American boy leaving Harlem for the Wild West. One book will tell you about the life of the famous African-American leader Malcolm X. Another book will take you right inside the terror of the Vietnam War. No matter which Walter Dean Myers books you read, you will become part of a tradition of storytelling. This tradition began on Herbert Dean's lap and carried on through the pen of Walter Dean Myers.

Chapter Two

GROWING UP IN HARLEM

On August 12, 1940, Walter Milton Myers celebrated his third birthday in Martinsburg, West Virginia. Helping him celebrate were his four sisters, Geraldine, Ethel, Viola, and Gertrude, and his two brothers, Douglas and George. His parents, Mary Green Myers and George Ambrose Myers, were there, too. Mrs. Myers was expecting another baby.

The Myers family was poor. With seven children and another one coming, it was hard for the family to make ends meet. Then, that same summer that Walter turned three, tragedy struck the family. Mary Green Myers died during the birth of her baby, Imogene.

Now there were eight children—and no mother. Mr. Myers tried to care for his children all by himself, but it was too difficult. George Myers could not earn money and be a father to his children at the same time. Luckily, friends stepped in to help. A couple named Herbert and Florence Dean offered to take some of the Myers children into their home and raise them. Even though the Deans had their own children, they wanted to help the Myers family.

Soon Walter and two of his sisters left Martinsburg with Mr. and Mrs. Dean. Their destination was Harlem. Walter remembers that he arrived in Harlem "with a snotty nose and wearing a pair of my sister's socks." Harlem became his home for the next 12 years, and the Deans became his foster parents. Foster parents are people who take care of a child when his or her birth parents cannot. The Deans took good care of young Walter and filled his life with love. Walter soon thought of them as his real parents.

Walter Myers, shown here at age four with one of his sisters, found a loving foster home with the Dean family in New York City's Harlem.

Walter's foster father, Herbert Dean, was always a great storyteller. Here, Herbert Dean poses with Walter's sons, Christopher (left) and Michael, in 1980.

Florence Dean was the daughter of a Native-American father and a German mother. She worked in a factory and also did housekeeping in other people's homes. Walter called Florence "Mother" or "Mama." Herbert Julius Dean had grown up in Baltimore, Maryland, where his father owned a small business. Herbert's grandfather, who owned land in Virginia, had been born a slave. Herbert himself had only gone to school through the third grade, but he was very bright and curious. He worked as a shipping clerk and handyman for the United States Radium Corporation. Walter and his sisters did not call Herbert "Father." Instead, they just called him "Herbert."

Walter Myers was very close to his foster mother.

Herbert was afraid that Walter would become a "mama's boy," but neither Mama nor Walter cared what he thought. Walter's sisters teased Mama, saying that she should "marry" Walter because she loved him so much. To Walter, Florence's love was very welcome. His own mother's death had been a huge loss, and Walter loved Florence's attention and her caring ways.

Walter was a very smart boy. His interest in reading and writing began at a young age. When he was four, Mama taught Walter to read, even though she could barely read herself. "I remember having her read to me every day from *True Romance* magazine," Walter recalls. *True Romance* was a magazine filled with romantic stories about love and marriage. Walter might not have been very interested in these subjects, but listening to Mama read aloud gave him a love for reading. In fact, by the time Walter was five, he was able to read the daily newspaper to Mama. Sometimes Mama also told stories. Many of her stories were about princes and princesses. Other stories were about real people such as Shirley Temple, a popular child actress, or Bessie Smith, a great blues singer.

Herbert Dean, however, was the main storyteller of the house. Many evenings Herbert would put Walter on his knee and begin to tell stories to the boy. Sometimes Herbert's tales of ghosts and strange creatures coming out of the sea at night were too much for Walter. It was especially frightening when Herbert pretended he was scared himself!

One day, Herbert told a story about a huge bunny that escaped from a farm and went around looking for naughty children. When Herbert got to the part about the bunny coming up the fire escape, he looked toward the window, pretended to be terrified, and ran down the hall and out of the building. Walter was right behind him!

Walter could also find plenty of stories just walking down the streets of Harlem. Harlem is a community in the northern part of the island of Manhattan, in New York City. Like many cities, New York was segregated. That meant people and neighborhoods were often separated by race. Nearly all of the people who lived in Harlem were African-American. There were rich people and poor people. They worked as doctors, maids, lawyers, janitors, teachers, ministers, artists, writers, dancers, and musicians.

Since about 1912, Harlem had been a gathering place for thousands of African Americans in the arts. Writers like Langston Hughes and Zora Neale Hurston lived and worked there. Singers such as Billie Holiday and Bessie Smith sang in clubs there. Ossie Davis and Ruby Dee, who are married and still acting today, began their stage careers in Harlem theaters. Harlem was spilling over with great talent. It was a lively, close-knit community.

On Sundays, Walter was picked up by his Sunday school teacher. Along with all the other Sunday school students, they walked down St. Nicholas Avenue to

Langston Hughes, one of the greatest African-American writers, was one of many inspiring figures in the Harlem of Walter Dean Myers's childhood.

their church. Other families thought Sundays were special, too. They would put on their finest clothes and stroll down Seventh Avenue, the widest street in Harlem. Like most of the neighborhood kids, Walter also went to Bible school. During the summer, Walter went to Bible school every day except Saturday, as well as to Sunday school.

Walter Myers loved living in Harlem. He loved the people, the places, and all the life going on around him. "I remember the bright sun on Harlem streets, the easy rhythms of black and brown bodies, the sounds of children streaming in and out of red-brick tenements," Walter recalled. Harlem was a place rich with talented, loving people. It is a place Walter has never forgotten.

Chapter *Three*

READING MAKES A WRITER

Because he could read well, young Walter Myers was a good student. He enjoyed what he learned at Public School 125 in Harlem. However, he soon found that he did not really fit in.

Walter had trouble speaking. He had the words in his head, but he had a hard time saying them. People often could not understand what he was saying. There were many words he could not pronounce, no matter how hard he tried. Other children in school laughed at the way Walter spoke. This hurt his feelings and he got into a lot of fights. Lonely and angry, Walter found his escape through reading. He read everything he could find, especially comic books. While he was reading, he was safe. No one could bother him.

Still, reading did not solve Walter's problems with other kids. In the fifth grade, Walter was suspended for fighting in class. His teacher, Mrs. Conway, told him to sit in the back of the class to wait for his mother.

Walter Myers in 1942.

While he waited, Walter secretly read a comic book under his desk. Mrs. Conway caught him. She grabbed his comic book and tore it up. Walter was upset. How could she take away his one comfort? Later, Mrs. Conway surprised Walter. She brought him a pile of her own books. She told Walter that if he was going to read, he might as well read something good. "That was the best thing that ever happened to me," Walter says.

Mrs. Conway's help did not end there. Children often had to stand in front of the class and read aloud from books. This made Walter nervous. His speech problem got even worse. Then Mrs. Conway made a new rule: If children wanted to, they could write some-

Walter Myers enjoyed growing up in the community of Harlem and playing in its streets and parks.

thing of their own to read to the class. Walter was relieved. When he wrote his own stories, he did not have to use words he could not pronounce! It was also easier for him to express himself on paper. So Walter began to write poems and short stories. Classmates who had laughed at him now praised his work.

Outside of school, Walter had a lot of fun in his Harlem neighborhood. His closest friend was Eric Leonhardt, a German-American boy. Walter also loved to play sports. He was big and tall and was good at any kind of ball game. In the church basement gym, he learned to play basketball. "Everyone in the neighborhood had a flat jump shot because of the low ceiling in the church gym," he remembered. The neighborhood children also played handball against the church wall, and baseball in a sandlot on Morningside Avenue.

Walter also spent a lot of time at the public library on 125th Street, in the heart of Harlem. Walter was happy to discover that what he enjoyed most was free. At the library he could read all the books he wanted without paying a penny! Through reading, Walter learned about other places, other times, and other people.

Walter attended Stuyvesant High School in downtown Manhattan. Stuyvesant was one of the best high schools in New York City. By this time, Walter had decided that he very much wanted to go to college. Then he found out that his parents could not afford to send him to college. This news was a big disappointment and very painful for Walter.

Another thing that hurt Walter was racism. His friend Eric began to get invited to parties, but Walter did not. He was left out because he was black. Walter began to feel more and more depressed. "What is the use of being bright if that brightness won't lead me where I want to go?" Walter wondered. At 15, he stopped going to school. He spent most of his time reading. For Walter, books were an escape from a world he felt had turned him away. Soon, however, he realized that staying out of school would only hurt him. Walter returned to Stuyvesant High School.

It was a good thing he did. One of his teachers, Miss Liebow, told him he was a gifted writer. She made up a list of important books that she thought Walter should read. Once again, a caring teacher was taking Walter under her wing. Walter borrowed the books from the library and read them hungrily. He also began to write short stories.

Yet Walter was still confused about his future. He had read books about writers and their lives. He began to imagine becoming a writer. Then he started entering his writing in contests, and he won prizes. Herbert and Florence Dean were happy that he won, but they did not understand how writing stories could help Walter's future. Racism and unfair laws in the United States made it hard for black people to get decent jobs—even if they had earned an education. To Walter's parents, hard work was the only way a young African American could survive on his own.

Walter understood his parents' point of view. Most of the black men he knew had low-paying jobs. He could see his friends' frustration. He could hear it in the stories they told, and he could feel it when they taunted him for "always having his head in a book." Walter was afraid that being black meant that his future would be hard. The idea of not going to college still bothered him. Once again, he became depressed.

Up until this time, Walter had done his best to be good. Now he stopped going to school again. This upset his parents very much. Where was this bright yet frustrated boy headed? The answer came to Walter while reading the war poems of Rupert Brooke, a poet who fought in World War I. On his 17th birthday, in 1954, Walter joined the United States Army. He did not tell his parents the news until the morning he left. Mama burst into tears. Herbert did not understand, but he gave Walter his blessing. Walter Myers walked out the door into the unknown.

Walter Dean Myers received encouragement for his writing from a teacher at Stuyvesant High School. This public high school is one of the finest in New York.

Chapter Four

BECOMING A WRITER

Walter spent three years in the U.S. Army. His experience there was not very rewarding. "I spent most of my time in the service playing basketball," Walter recalled. "I also learned several efficient ways of killing human beings."

When he got out of the Army at the age of twenty, Walter's problems were still not solved. He still had a speech problem, and he did not have any job skills. Walter moved back in with his parents. By then they had moved to Morristown, New Jersey, in the suburbs outside of New York City. Walter got a job in a nearby factory, loading trucks. Later, he worked at the post office unloading the mail chute. He hated his jobs, but at least his books and notebooks were always close by. At night, he wrote. But life in Morristown was not keeping Walter happy. He moved back to New York City. Shortly after that, he met and married his first wife, Joyce.

Walter Myers spent three years in the U.S. Army. Afterward, he still dreamed of becoming a writer.

Unfortunately, Walter was soon fired from his job at the post office. After that, he worked as a messenger, and later as a clerk in a factory. He did not like those jobs, either, but he was still writing. He also found happiness through the birth of his daughter, Karen, and son, Michael Dean.

While busy with family life and working, Walter was still trying to establish himself as a writer. For a while he hung out with other artists, who were using drugs and alcohol. This led to an unhappy end to his marriage with Joyce. How could Walter get his life

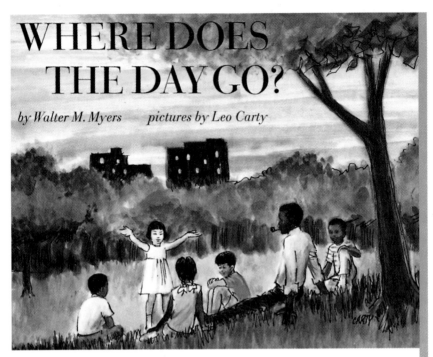

WHERE DOES THE DAY GO?

by Walter M. Myers   *pictures by Leo Carty*

Where Does the Day Go? won a special contest for African-American writers. In 1969, it became Walter Myers's first published book.

together? Once again, writing was the answer. He focused himself even more on his writing and began sending his work to magazines. Walter knew that every poem or story that was published increased his chance of success as a writer. The more he published, the more people would recognize his name. Soon, Walter's work was showing up in men's adventure magazines, Sunday newspaper magazines, and even mystery magazines. His work was also published in black magazines like *The Liberator*, *Black World*, and *Negro Digest*. Still, this young man was not satisfied.

He wanted to do something with his writing, something important. He wanted to write things that reflected who he was and where he came from.

One day in 1968, Walter Myers learned that a group called the Council on Interracial Books for Children was having a contest. It was a special contest for black writers of children's books. Walter had never thought of writing for children, but he was eager to write anything. Walter wrote a short story and entered it into the contest. The story was called *Where Does the Day Go?* In it, a father and a group of children go for a walk in the park just before sundown. "Where does the day go?" one child asks. Karen thinks the day breaks up into little pieces and becomes stars. Kiku thinks the day slides into the ocean, and José believes it fills people's eyes and makes them sleepy. They all discuss each idea. Then the father provides the real explanation of why there is day and night. *Where Does the Day Go?* won the special contest, and was published as a picture book in 1969. The prize was a big break in Walter's writing career.

In 1970, when he was 33 years old, Walter got another break. He was hired as an **editor** for the Bobbs-Merrill Publishing Company. Publishing companies, or **publishers**, make authors' stories into books so they can be sold. Bobbs-Merrill felt that it needed a black editor, because it had none at the time. Walter had no experience editing, but another writer convinced Walter to take the position. His job would be to work with writers to make their books as good as possible.

"I had this enormous desk, in this enormous office," he later explained. Walter soon began learning about the publishing business. He learned just how and why books and authors are chosen to be published. He learned that books are not published just because they are good. They also have to be able to sell! One of the first authors Walter worked with was Nikki Giovanni, an African-American poet. He edited her first book of **prose**, *Gemini*.

Walter's new job as an editor did not stop him from writing. Nothing could. He wrote articles for magazines and two more picture books: *The Dancers*, and *Fly, Jimmy, Fly!* The characters in those books were named after his children and other members of his family. When he wrote *Fly, Jimmy, Fly!* Walter changed his name from Walter Milton Myers to Walter Dean Myers. This was to honor his foster parents, Florence and Herbert Dean.

The Dancers is about a boy named Michael. One day, Michael's father takes him to see the ballet. Michael invites the ballerina to visit him, but she cannot come. Then, one day, she arrives at Michael's house with her partner, who is a violinist. They perform in the street, and all the children begin dancing, too. Afterward, everyone goes to Michael's house for dinner. Michael and his friend Karen teach the ballerina to dance a popular dance called the Funky Chicken.

In 1973, a year after *The Dancers* was published,

Walter Dean Myers married again. His new wife, Constance Brendel, was called Connie. Walter was determined not to make the same kinds of mistakes he had made in his first marriage. Before long, Connie and Walter celebrated the birth of a son, Christopher.

Around this time, Walter met another editor, who had read one of his short stories. The editor thought the short story was the first chapter of a novel and asked how the rest of the novel went. Even though it was not a novel, Walter quickly thought of how the story might continue. He described it to the editor. Right on the spot, he was offered a contract to write the novel! A contract is a written agreement that writers make with publishers.

Fast Sam, Cool Clyde, and Stuff was published as a novel in 1975. This book was different from his earlier books. It was for young teenagers instead of young children. Books written for this age are called **young adult books**. Walter again turned to his own life for this story. *Fast Sam, Cool Clyde, and Stuff* is told by Stuff, who is remembering when he was a 13-year-old living in Harlem. Stuff and his friends lived in a world of broken homes, problems with the police, street fights, sex, and drugs. In order to cope, they formed a gang called the Good People. The book's humor was a light way of looking back at Walter's own childhood

Walter Dean Myers became known for writing books about teenagers, especially African-American teenagers. Here, he poses with his own young son, Christopher.

and at the many challenges of growing up in Harlem.

Fast Sam, Cool Clyde, and Stuff received many compliments from book reviewers. Book reviewers are people who comment on new books. They praised the way Walter made the language sound so natural. Reviewers also liked the positive way he portrayed inner-city youth. One reviewer wrote, "One of the nicest things about the book is that it is so hopeful." Although the kids in the story "live near drugs and welfare checks," the book shows their strength and humor. Walter knew there was a lot more material where this story came from. Walter Dean Myers was getting closer and closer to writing about the world he knew so well.

Chapter *Five*

POSITIVE IMAGES

Now that his work was getting attention, Walter Dean Myers wanted to write about what was most important to him. He had never been happy with the way African Americans were shown in books. He had the same feeling about the way they were shown in movies and on television. "Blacks were portrayed as nonserious people," he wrote. Walter looked back on his own childhood. All the important people he ever learned about—writers, presidents, scientists—had been white.

As his books became popular, Walter realized that he had a new role. As a black writer, he wanted his books to include African-American children as main characters. These books would tell about the way black children live. They would give the positive message that African-American children can succeed no matter what obstacles they face. Walter Dean Myers decided that he would write stories that would make

YOUNG MARTIN'S PROMISE

by Walter Dean Myers
Alex Haley, General Editor

Walter Dean Myers writes fiction with strong, realistic African-American characters. He has also written nonfiction about black heroes like Martin Luther King, Jr.

African-American children proud of their heritage.

In 1977, Walter met an obstacle of his own. There were big changes at the Bobbs-Merrill Publishing Company, and many people there lost their jobs. Walter was one of them. He had been working there for seven years. Now his job as an editor was gone. Fortunately, he had a contract to write another young adult novel. That made him feel better, and it meant that there was still money coming in. Then, Walter sat down with his wife, Connie, and together they came up with an idea. What if Walter did not even look for another job? What if he tried to make a living as a full-time writer? The idea was scary, but very exciting! Walter decided to go for it.

At first, Walter continued to write a lot of magazine articles, especially sports articles for men's magazines. Some of his assignments took him to fascinating places. Magazine editors sent him to Peru to write about bullfighting and to Japan to write about kick boxing. He also went to Colombia to write about the Quechua, one of the native peoples of that country. Walter took his family with him every chance he got. Together they enjoyed seeing the world. These travel experiences also helped Walter come up with ideas for future stories. In fact, almost all of his experiences found their way into his books. Whenever he came

Walter Dean Myers traveled the world to write articles. He often took his family. Here, Connie, Christopher, and Walter visit Bangkok, Thailand.

upon a new situation at home or abroad, he would ask himself, "What if…?" and let his imagination wander.

Before long, his "what if…?" would become a novel. For instance, once Walter and his family were looking for a new place to live in New York City. Walter went to see some old buildings the city was selling. The buildings were extremely cheap—some cost only $25! But that was because the buildings were in terrible condition. Walter wondered: What would happen if some teenagers bought a building like that? His question became the starting point for his next book, *The Young Landlords*. In this book, a group of teenagers becomes the owners of a run-down apartment building. Through their adventures, they learn about relationships between landlords (those who own buildings) and tenants (those who pay rent to live in them). The teens also learn about friendship and hard work. *The Young Landlords* became very popular and was later made into a film.

Over the next 15 years, Walter wrote almost 50 more books for young people. He became known for writing about the lives of black youth in the inner city, especially in Harlem. Walter's novels have never hidden the truth. They show the real struggles that teenagers living in rough neighborhoods must deal with. Walter captures the way African Americans, both children and young adults, speak, move, and live. He also writes in detail about their surroundings so that his readers can feel that they are there with the characters.

Not all of Walter Dean Myers's books, however, are about the inner city. Some are adventure stories set in faraway places such as ancient Africa. The titles of these exciting books include *The Legend of Tarik*, *The Hidden Shrine*, and *Ambush in the Amazon*. Walter has also written nonfiction books, such as *Malcolm X: By Any Means Necessary*. This is the life story of Malcolm X, an important leader of the Civil Rights Movement. To Walter Dean Myers, it is important that young African Americans know about their history and the heroes who created it.

Walter has written about African-American history in some unusual ways. *Brown Angels: An Album of Pictures and Verse* is Walter's first book of poems. The poems were written to go with photographs of black children from the early 1900s. Walter spent many years collecting these photos. "I found the first one in a flea market," Walter explained. "I picked up the first one, then the second and third. Now I have well over one thousand pictures."

Still, Walter's greatest love is putting pieces of his own life into the novels he writes. For instance, Walter has always written about basketball because he has played the game all his life. His book *Hoops*, published in 1981, is narrated by 17-year-old Lonnie, who is a good basketball player. Lonnie and his coach are friends—but both are under pressure to lose the championship on purpose. If they throw the game, some people will make a lot of money on bets. In the end, Lonnie learns there are rough people in the business of basketball. If he wants to become a pro, he'll have to cope with them. Walter may never have had this exact experience, but he did know about the world of basketball and the importance of sticking up for yourself.

In his book *The Mouse Rap*, published in 1990, Walter begins each chapter with a rap verse by the book's main character, who is named Mouse. Mouse's summer activities in Harlem are filled with fun and

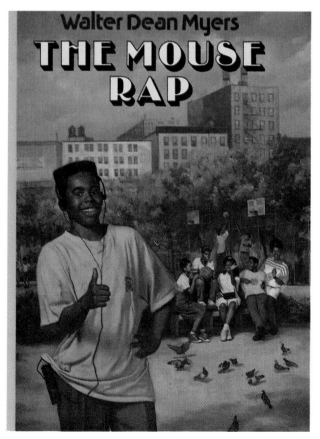

The Mouse Rap captures the fun and the challenges of growing up in Harlem.

mischief. Sometimes he dodges his father and the duties that are waiting for him. One day he enters a dance contest. Mouse even goes searching for a dead mobster's hidden loot! All these episodes hint of Walter's own Harlem childhood—from skipping school, to entering writing contests, to hanging out with the wrong crowd.

One of Walter's more serious books is *Fallen Angels*. It is the story of American soldiers fighting in the Vietnam War. Walter himself did not go to Vietnam, but his Army experience helped him write the book.

Walter Dean Myers won several awards for his powerful story of young soldiers in Vietnam, *Fallen Angels*.

Walter felt that it was important for him to write *Fallen Angels*, so that teenagers could see both the horror of war and a troubled part of U.S. history. *Fallen Angels* won several awards, including the Coretta Scott King Author Award. This award is named for Coretta Scott King, a civil rights activist and the widow of Martin Luther King, Jr.

Walter's interest in history also helped him write *The Glory Field*, published in 1994. This book begins in 1753 with young Muhammad Bilal's journey from Africa to the American colonies. It ends in the 1990's with a family holding a reunion on the plantation where Muhammad, their ancestor, was enslaved.

What makes Walter Dean Myers books so special to young readers? Using plain language and beautiful story-telling, Walter tries to show black teenagers that if they can dream about something, they can achieve it.

Achieving your dreams, however, takes a lot of hard work. Walter Dean Myers knows this from personal experience. He pursued his dream of becoming a writer, even when it seemed impossible to achieve. Even today, Walter must work hard to keep himself writing. He gets up every morning between four-thirty and five o'clock, and he takes a five-mile walk until about seven o'clock. This wakes him up and warms him. Then, after a shower, he starts to work. He tries to write ten pages every day.

Walter has a set way for writing a book. First, he outlines the story. Then, he writes the first draft very

Walter Dean Myers sometimes finds inspiration in his many collections, including his collections of old photographs.

quickly. After that, he begins rewriting. The rewriting stage takes a lot of time and thought. Walter admits that he never feels completely finished with his work. He seldom reads his books after they are published. He says, "It always bothers me to read them because I always see something I should have changed!"

This author becomes inspired to write his books when he travels to different cities. "I need to get out of the familiar to get into the setting of a book," he says. Traveling also helps Walter with his hobby, which is collecting interesting old objects. He loves going to flea markets, junk shops, and secondhand shops. Sometimes he even searches through dumpsters! One collection Walter is very proud of is his collection of over three thousand black history books. Another is his collection of family photos and his photographs of black children from the early 1900s that inspired *Brown Angels*.

Looking back on his life, Walter can say that he overcame most of the obstacles he faced—even his speech problem. When he was nearly thirty, Walter found a special way to cope with this problem. He heard about someone who had a stutter, but who got over it by speaking in a different accent. The next time Walter had to speak in front of a crowd, he tried talking with an accent—and it worked! Now, Walter Dean Myers continues to travel all over the country making speeches. He has come a long way from the painful days of standing in front of Mrs. Conway's class!

Chapter **Six**

A WRITER'S COMMITMENT

Today, Walter Dean Myers still works hard. He also still speaks up for and to young African Americans. He wants to make sure black children can look in a book and see themselves. He wants to give black children the message "You are beautiful!"

Because of his strong talent and his commitment to writing for children, most of the fifty books Walter Dean Myers has written have won awards. In fact, Walter has won some awards several times! In addition to the Coretta Scott King Author Award, Walter has won many other awards from the American Library Association. His books have also been named Newbery Honor Book and School Library Journal Best Book of the Year.

These awards have helped make Walter Dean Myers a popular author. He is often invited to share his knowledge and experiences with others. When he has time, Myers speaks before writers' groups or

Walter Dean Myers has always received support and inspiration from his family and his community. Here, Walter is joined by his son Christopher, sister Imogene, wife Connie, and sister Ethel.

teaches on a part-time basis. He has taught African-American literature and creative writing to high school students. These classrooms are great places to discover some of that language he uses in his books.

Walter's life experience has not only helped him write books, it has also helped him get a college degree. Normally, it takes four years to finish college. Sometimes, though, people can get credit for work they do outside of the classroom. Walter Dean Myers began at Empire State College in 1983 and finished only one year later. How did he do it? He got "life experience" credits for three years! That means that

SCORPIONS
BY WALTER DEAN MYERS

Many young people relate their own lives to the lives of the characters in books like *Scorpions*.

Walter had done so much important work on his own that the college felt it was equal to three years' worth of studying in college.

Through those years of experience, Walter Dean Myers has had a lot to say to young readers. But what do the readers of Walter's books have to say to him? Walter gets letters from young readers all over the country. In these letters, readers tell how Walter's books have touched their lives.

One reader wrote to Walter after reading his book *Scorpions*, about a young boy who learns the value of strength and friendship while growing up in Harlem. The reader told Walter about his own experiences growing up in the city "with gangs on every corner."

Another young reader commented on *Hoops*, a book about the challenges faced by a young basketball player who dreams of a pro career. He told Walter that all the characters in the book "sound real." When he read *Hoops*, the reader said, "I imagined myself playing basketball with all my friends, and talking like the characters in the book."

Many of the young people who write to Walter say that they did not like to read—until they discovered Walter's books. "Reading this book makes me want to read more," said one letter. Another reader told Walter that now, instead of hanging out or playing basketball every afternoon, "I have better things to do—read one of your books."

It is clear from these letters that Walter Dean Myers has achieved his goal. Young people everywhere can see themselves in his books. Yet Walter says he will never stop writing. "As a black writer, I want to talk about my people," he says. And more and more ideas for books keep coming to him. "There is always one more story to tell," he says, "one more person whose life needs to be held up to the sun."

Walter Dean Myers believes that his writing is a way of reaching out to other people. He is especially happy when young African Americans find hope and encouragement in his books. Through his writing,

Walter hopes to pass something on to a new generation of black people. "If each generation has to start all over again, you are fighting the same battle as your grandfather," he says.

At the same time, Walter will never forget the gifts he received from his own family and community. They gave him the courage to dream and to achieve. They also gave him many of his stories. Nearly fifty years after he heard his first stories on Herbert Dean's knee, Walter talked about his family's legacy of storytelling. Both his father and his grandfather had dropped out of school after the third grade, and neither one was much of a reader. Yet one day, Walter told Herbert Dean about a story he was writing, and Herbert asked Walter to repeat the story. It turned out to be a story that Herbert had told Walter years before—and Herbert said he had heard the story from his own grandfather! Walter was the first one to write down and publish these stories, but many had been in his family for generations. The experience helped Walter realize something. "I'm the same kind of person as my father, and his father before him," he said.

It has been a long journey for Walter Dean Myers from Martinsburg, West Virginia, to Harlem, and finally to Jersey City, New Jersey, where he and his family live today. He has been through loss, frustration, and many uphill climbs. But perhaps the title of one of his more recent books speaks for Walter's triumph. It is called *Now Is Your Time! The African-American Struggle for*

After publishing more than fifty books, Walter Dean Myers still has many more stories to tell.

Freedom. When it won the 1992 Coretta Scott King Author Award, the judges said that it was "truly a gift to readers of the new generation." The same can be said for its author. Walter Dean Myers is truly a gift to young readers and writers everywhere.

Important Dates

1937   Born Walter Milton Myers on August 12, in Martinsburg, West Virginia.

1940   Mother dies. Taken in by Herbert and Florence Dean, who raise him in Harlem, New York.

1954   Joins the U.S. Army.

1957   Discharged from the Army. Returns to New York City.

1968   Wins the Council on Interracial Books for Children Award for *Where Does the Day Go?*

1969   *Where Does the Day Go?* is published as a picture book. It is the first of over fifty books he will write for children and young adults.

1970   Becomes an editor at Bobbs-Merrill, a publishing company.

1973   Marries Constance Brendel.

1975   Publishes first young adult novel, *Fast Sam, Cool Clyde, and Stuff.*

1977   Loses job at Bobbs-Merrill. Becomes a full-time writer.

1984   Receives a B.A. from Empire State College.

1993   Publishes first book of poems, *Brown Angels.*

Glossary

fiction   Stories that come from the author's imagination.

editor   A person in a publishing house who recommends which new books should be published. Editors also work with authors to help improve their writing.

nonfiction   A true story, report, article, or interview that is based on actual fact, researched or reported by the author.

novels   Long, fictional stories that fill a whole book.

picture books   Books for young children that have few words but have illustrations on every page.

prose   Writing that is not poetry.

publishers   Companies that prepare and manufacture books for sale.

young adult books   Books for readers aged 12 and older.

Bibliography

Myers, Walter Dean. *Brown Angels: An Album of Pictures and Verse*. New York: HarperCollins, 1993.

Myers, Walter Dean. *The Mouse Rap*. New York: HarperCollins, 1990.

Myers, Walter Dean, *Now Is Your Time! The African-American Struggle for Freedom*. New York: HarperCollins, 1991.

Index